Reiki

The Complete Beginners Guide To This Ancient Healing Process: Heal, Energize And Inspire!

By Sarah Gemson

Respective authors own all copyrights not held by the publisher.

The information herein is offered for informational purposes solely, and is universal as so. The presentation of the information is without contract or any type of guarantee assurance.

The trademarks that are used are without any consent, and the publication of the trademark is without permission or backing by the trademark owner. All trademarks and brands within this book are for clarifying purposes only and are the owned by the owners themselves, not affiliated with this document.

Disclaimer – Please read!

The information provided in this book is designed to provide helpful information on the subjects discussed. This book is not meant to be used, nor should it be used, to diagnose or treat any medical condition. For diagnosis or treatment of any medical problem, consult your own physician. The publisher and author are not responsible for any specific health or allergy needs that may require medical supervision and are not liable for any damages or negative consequences from any treatment, action, application or preparation, to any person reading or following the information in this book. References are provided for informational purposes only and do not constitute endorsement of any websites or other sources. Readers should be aware that the websites listed in this book may change.

Table of Contents

Introduction

If you are reading this book, then you have already been introduced to the concept of Reiki. Maybe you have a friend, family member, or co-worker who has tried it. Perhaps you have tried it yourself and now you are intrigued and want to learn more about this ancient healing practice. Whether you believe you just stumbled onto Reiki or you believe that fate brought it into your life, you have now been put onto a path that you just can't ignore.

Many of the traditional forms of healing developed in the Far East thousands of years ago have been brought to the west, often shrouded in mysticism. Yet, these forms of healing have drawn the interest of many westerners because they offer a peaceful, gentle means of healing the body, mind, and soul, of realigning oneself with the energy of the universe. Reiki is one of these forms of healing. Originally practiced in Tibet thousands of years ago, the practice of Reiki was rediscovered in the late 1800s/early 1900s by Dr. Mikao Usui, a Japanese Buddhist monk.

Dr. Usui first considered the concept of Reiki when a college student he was teaching asked him how Jesus managed to perform his healing miracles. The question set Dr. Usui on a quest to find the answer. Dr. Usui traveled extensively, ending up in the mountains of Kori Yama, where he meditated and fasted for 21 days. The result of this quiet and peaceful time was spiritual enlightenment and the acquired ability to heal – Reiki Ryoho.

Over the rest of his lifetime, Dr. Usui taught Reiki to more than 2,000 people, including Dr. Chujiro Hayashi, who developed the modern healing form of Reiki. Mrs. Hawayo Takata learned Reiki from Dr. Hayashi when she travelled from Hawaii to Japan to find treatment for health problems that plagued her. She then brought the practice of Reiki to North America when she returned.

Reiki literally means Universal Life Energy. It is a word created from two Japanese words – Rei means "Universal Life" and Ki means "Energy." Reiki is a form of energy work. It involves the use of touch as a method of directing life force energy into the body to balance the spiritual, mental, emotional, and physical energies within the body. This does sounds a lot like what Jesus did when he healed people with the laying-on-of-hands, but while Reiki deals with energy and the healing of the spirit, it is not itself aligned with any specific spiritual doctrine.

Anyone, anywhere who is ready to open themselves to the wonderful healing Reiki offers can practice this ancient form of healing. Once you have opened yourself to it, you will be forever changed. It is wonderful practiced on its own or acts to complement other types of treatment, conventional and traditional.

I hope you are excited about the journey ahead, as you fully explore the healing practice of Reiki in this beginners guide. You will learn how Reiki *is* the energy that is all around us and you will be guided through the five principles of this healing practice. Then you will lean how Reiki can heal the body, mind, and soul and the various techniques used to accomplish this healing. Finally, for those of you whose interest is piqued enough to want to learn the practice of Reiki, there is an introduction to Reiki training and attunement.

Welcome to this wonderful journey!

Chapter 1: The Reiki-Energy Connection

Universal Energy

The entire universe is filled with a life force energy that is constantly flowing everywhere at once. In fact, the universe *IS* energy! *Matter* is energy! *We* are energy! This energy is flowing through each and every one of us, around us, and connects us to each other and every other part of the universe. Just imagine being connected by this amazing energy to something – or someone! – at the other side of the universe.

How does this energy flow through us? There are different opinions regarding this. There are people who believe that the energy flows into us from above, through the top of our head, the location of the crown chakra. There are others who think that the energy flows into us from the earth through our root chakra. Still others believe this energy flows into us via the tan tien (pronounced "dawn tea in"), which is located about 2 ½ inches below the naval and is considered to be the center of our individual power or ki. It is also possible that this energy or Reiki flows into the body in a way that combines all three of these options.

Unfortunately, there are times in life when there are blocks within us, blocks that don't allow this energy to flow through as it is meant to. These energy blocks form within us throughout our life due to experiences we have and the emotions that come out of those experiences. These could be traumatic childhood experiences and/or things that happen to us later in life. The more we either consciously or unconsciously accept negative emotions, which then become attached to the energy flow, the more we disrupt and reduce that flow of energy through the body. This disrupts our ability to feel positive emotions. The flow of energy through us can slow down to the point that it comes to a standstill. If this goes on for a long period of time, physical illness can result.

Reiki

Reiki is the ability of the practitioner to tap into this Universal Life Force energy and direct it to flow into the body. Again, Rei is Universal Life and Ki is Energy. Thus, Reiki *is* Universal Life Energy. This is the energy that causes the formation of galaxies, solar systems, stars, and planets and it is the energy that creates all life on Earth, including our own. Every person has Universal Life Energy or Reiki flowing through them.

As we discussed above, the flow of this energy enters the body. The Reiki practitioner holds her hands in position on the body of the recipient and the energy flows through the practitioner's hands and into the body. The speed of flow depends on how much blockage there is, how severe the illness is, and how ready the recipient is to change. Of course, since Reiki is Universal Life Force energy, there is an unlimited source of it. The flow of it can literally go on forever. In this chapter, we will discuss how Reiki feels and further on we will discuss how to use it for the purpose of healing both ourselves and others.

How Reiki Feels

Reiki feels different for each person that gives and receives it and it can even feel different from one treatment session to another. Most recipients will feel nothing other than the actual touch of the practitioner's hands on their body. However, there are a few people who, when receiving a treatment, have a higher sensitivity to the energy and will feel other sensations.

These sensations might come across as nothing more than a temperature difference. The practitioner's hands might feel cold, warm, or even hot. But it is also possible to feel something more, such as the feeling of tingling, vibrations, numbness, itchiness, chills, or throbbing. There have even been instances where the recipient has felt extra sets of hands on her body, which has been interpreted by some to be spirit guides joining in. Fortunately, Reiki works just fine, whether or not the recipient feels anything at all.

The Reiki practitioner can also feel various sensations when working with a recipient, particularly in the hands. Hands can feel hot or cold. The temperature felt in the hands can change during the treatment session as the practitioner moves her hands from one part of the recipient's body to another. The recipient can feel the practitioner's hands as being hot while at the same time the practitioner's hands feel cold to her. The opposite can also be the case.

Pulsating energy is another feeling that is common in Reiki practitioners. While it can be felt anywhere in the body, it is most commonly felt in the hands because the hands are the conduit for the flow of energy. Because Reiki is the Universal

Life Force energy, its natural state is to flow anywhere and everywhere. When the Reiki practitioner is attuned and near someone, the energy sometimes wants to begin flowing, causing it to collect in the palms of the hands, waiting for release. There is nothing wrong with this. You can place your hands on yourself if this happens to you, allowing the Reiki to flow into your body. You can also place your hands on someone nearby, but only if you have permission to do so. Otherwise, just let Reiki flow from you as it will. It can still reach people who are near you.

There may be times after you are attuned to Reiki that you will feel more than simply pulsating energy. You might feel balls of such pulsating energy that almost feel like solid, living things. These balls of energy can form in your hands and feel somewhat awkward, particularly when you are not performing a treatment. The reason these balls of energy form could simply be that your own body needs treatment. When you feel balls of energy in your hands, place your hands on your body and allow the energy to flow into you. This will help alleviate the energy buildup in your palms and heal you at the same time.

You can also use this balled up energy to infuse inanimate objects with Reiki. You can touch anything and fill it with Reiki, such as bathwater, candles, food, incense, clothing and shoes, and your bed and pillow. Having Reiki in these things will help you feel better when you use them.

If during a treatment session your hands begin to vibrate, it could be a simple matter of the recipient needing the energy so much that it is flowing fast. However, the surface area of your palms is not large, and if the energy is trying to flow through them faster than they can accommodate it, then your hands might begin to vibrate. This won't hurt you at all. If you ever experience any pain, which is rare, but can occur in the hand and wrist joints, you can pull back and take a rest. You can even do a treatment session where you alternate hands on for a few minutes and hands off for a few minutes.

Perhaps the most important thing to know about Reiki is that it follows the path of least resistance when it flows, just like water. When it flows into the body, it will flow along the energy channels that offer the least resistance. Remember the blocks we talked about above? When Reiki encounters these blocks, it might stop flowing, if the block is big and solid enough. If you find a place in the body where Reiki stops flowing, do not remove your hands right away. Sometimes just adjusting their position slightly one way or the other, side to side or up or down, will get the flow moving again. Sometimes you simply have to wait and keep your hands in position and the block might give way. Regardless, wait and hold your hands on the body for the standard five minutes and then move on, even if you still feel the blockage. This might be an area of the recipient that you have to visit more often.

Personal Energy vs. Reiki

As we discussed above, Reiki is Universal Life Force energy. This energy flows from the universe, through the practitioner and into the recipient. None of the practitioner's personal energy is being transferred into the recipient and the practitioner shouldn't feel drained afterward.

However, this is not to say that the personal energies of both the recipient and the practitioner do not interact with each other. The personal energies of any two people who are in close proximity to each other will merge. During a Reiki session, when the personal energies of the practitioner and the recipient come together it's called fusion, and while the feeling of it is often confused with that of Reiki, if you have become adept and experienced with energies and Reiki, then you may be able to distinguish the two. Essentially, the main difference is that personal energies are infused with emotion, whereas Reiki is not.

The Chakras and the Aura

The seven chakras and the aura are very important in the practice of Reiki. Even though the concept of the chakras originated in India, they are universal in their presence in the human body and they have been described by many different cultures around the world, perhaps by different names, but based on the same principles of energy centers in the body. For examples, the meridians in traditional Chinese medicine relate directly to the chakras.

The chakras are the energy centers of the body and the aura is the energy field that surrounds the body. Let's take a look at the chakras first. There are seven chakras in the human body, seven energy centers, which can be seen in the following diagram.

You will see later on, when we discuss the hand positions for Reiki, that these positions line up with the chakras, which is why an understanding of the chakras is important. Chakra is a Sanskrit word that means a wheel that spins on its own axis.

Each of the chakras in the body spins relative to the energy levels in your overall energy system. The chakras are as follows:

Root Chakra

Associated with the color red, this is also known as the first chakra. The root chakra is the energy that grounds us, that helps us connect to the energy of the earth. Children feel a connection with the birth mother or close family via the root chakra and it also serves as the root of our survival instincts. When this chakra is unbalanced, we are confused, disconnected, and distracted.

Sacral Chakra

Associated with the color orange, this is also known as the second chakra. The sacral chakra's energy is connected to our relationships with others, and in particular, control within those relationships. This chakra helps us to make changes in our lives through the personal choices we make. If this chakra is healthy and functioning properly, it ensures a balanced masculine/feminine energy or yin/yang.

Solar Plexus Chakra

Associated with the color yellow, this is also known as the third chakra. The solar plexus chakra is the energy associated with our intuition and our ego. The health of our self-esteem is determined by the health of the solar plexus chakra. When this chakra is blocked or not functioning properly, our intuitive skills will not work properly and we will struggle with our personal power.

Heart Chakra

Associated with the color green, this is also known as the fourth chakra. This is the chakra that is responsible for the love within our energy system and when the chakra is unbalanced we feel it deeply, often in the form of grief, heartbreak, and fear. Balancing the heart chakra is a very pure form of healing.

Throat Chakra

Associated with the color blue, this is also known as the fifth chakra. The throat chakra is the energy of our will. It is the center of our speech, which is the primary way we express ourselves to others and how healthy that expression of ourselves is signifies the health of this chakra. The throat chakra is diminished in energy each time we do not speak genuinely, but utter half-truths and lies, not speaking what we need to express. This includes not expressing anger and displeasure, but rather ignoring these emotions and repressing them. It is important to always speak up when we have something that must be said.

Brow Chakra

Associated with the color indigo, this is also known as the sixth chakra. This is where the third eye or mind center resides. The energy of this chakra is linked to our mental processes. This is where we evaluate our life and our experiences and it is from here that our wisdom comes. When this chakra is strong, we have the ability to distinguish fact from fantasy and perceive visual images around us, including the aura of others.

Crown Chakra

Associated with the color purple and with the color white, this is also known as the seventh chakra. The crown chakra is located at the top of the head and connects us with the spiritual energy of the universe. This is where many believe the Universal Life Force energy enters the body so that it can filter down through to the other six chakras. This is also the source of our intuitive knowledge.

The Aura

A person's aura is different from the chakras, although the two are connected. The aura is the energy field that surrounds a person's body and this energy field stems from the chakras. In fact, while each chakra is rooted in the physical body, the energy of each of the chakras extends into the aura, giving the aura seven distinct layers, in addition to the physical body. The vibrational energy of the aura increases with each level.

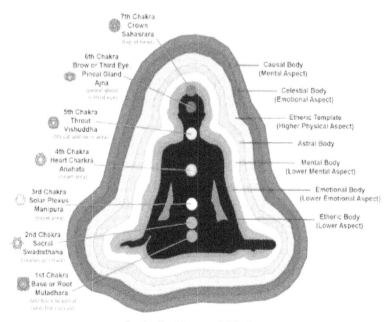

Auric Bodies and Chakras

The above image shows how the aura and the chakras relate to each other. The layers or bodies of the aura are as follows:

Physical Body: Our consciousness, who we are, is manifested in the here and now in the form of our physical body. This is the part of us that is associated with this life, the part that is born, ages, and dies.

Etheric Body: This is a layer that is red and is about 2 cm think and surrounds the physical body. This body is connected to the root chakra and it is through this body that the energy flows into the chakras of the physical body.

Emotional Body: This body is orange and surrounds the first two bodies. This body reflects all the feelings that we have and is connected to the sacral chakra.

Mental Body: This body is yellow and surrounds in the inner three bodies. It reflects the conscious mind and our ability to think and reason. This body is connected to the solar plexus chakra.

Astral Body: This body is green. It surrounds the inner four bodies and represents complete, unconditional love. It is connected to the heart chakra and it acts as the bridge between the physical and spiritual realms of existence.

Etheric Template Body: This body is blue. It surrounds the inner five bodies and represents memory and thought processes. It acts like a mirror for all of our memories, whether we actually remember them or have repressed or forgotten them. This body is also the vessel that stores within it the present and all possible futures. It is connected with the throat chakra.

Celestial Body: This body is indigo. It surrounds the inner six bodies and mirrors our subconscious mind. By tapping into our subconscious, this life can be easier and more enjoyable and rewarding. This body embodies universal love and is connected to the brow chakra.

Causal Body: This body is purple. It surrounds all the other bodies and the energy within it spins at an extremely high frequency. It connects the conscious mind to the soul via the subconscious mind. This body is the beginning of the creative impulse and is associated with all higher forms of knowledge. It is connected to the crown chakra.

Chapter 2: The Five Principles of Reiki

The Five Principles of Reiki were created by Dr. Usui. They are suggestions that he came up with on how to live life in a peaceful manner. The Five Principles of Reiki are:

Just for today, I let go of worry
Just for today, I let go of anger
Just for today, I will express gratitude
Just for today, I will do my work honestly
Just for today, I will be kind to my neighbor and every living thing

Anyone, whether they receive Reiki treatments, practice Reiki, or even know what Reiki is, can bring these five principles into their lives. Dr. Usui's goal behind the creation of these five principles was to bring awareness to the fact that we can only be truly healthy on a spiritual, mental, and physical level when we take responsibility for ourselves and our own wellbeing. Let's take a look at each of the Five Principles of Reiki in detail.

Just for today, I let go of worry:

Worry is a creation of our mind. It is a response to our inability to know what the future holds. In our mind, we can imagine what the future will be like and this imagining is based on our experiences and knowledge from the past. But what we imagine is not reality and will most likely never happen. Simply put, we cannot know what the future will be.

When we worry, we experience the emotions associated with something that has not happened. But because we feel the emotions every time we think of the thing we are worried about, it becomes difficult for us to see any other possibility. The result is that we create the future about which we have been worried.

Once we let go of worry, we are able to trust in ourselves and our ability to handle anything that might happen. This brings a state of peace that we can feel even in the midst of challenge. Any time we feel worried, we must remember that it is a state of mind, not reality, and that we are able to let it go if we choose to.

Just for today, I let go of anger:

Anger is nothing more than a reaction to a situation. It is not a response, not an action. Anger is something that is created by us, by our minds. When we feel anger, we get tense, our heart rate goes up, and our judgement is impaired. Anger is a negative energy, one that, when directed at someone else, can cause them to create anger that is directed back at us or at someone else. The more anger we create, the easier it is to create more anger.

Remember that letting go of anger is a choice, as is holding on to it. The key whenever we feel anger is to come to understand what it is that made us feel that way. We can choose to examine it and then we can choose to let the anger go and take action, if action is warranted or possible. This is how we moved forward, rather than becoming mired in the anger.

Just for today, I will express gratitude:

Expressing gratitude each day is not about being thankful for your job and your family and all the things in your life. Of course, these things are all important, but this level of gratitude is about understanding that everything you need for that day has been provided for you. This is gratitude for being alive, for our physical existence, for what we have brought into our own lives.

Just for today, I will do my work honestly:

This statement is not necessarily related to our daily work, the work that we do to support ourselves and our family, although this work is part of the larger picture. This statement refers to living an honest life by being true to ourselves and true to others. The only way we can build an honest, fulfilling life is if we do not hide from ourselves or others, but live openly and honestly the best way we are able.

Just for today, I will be kind to my neighbor and every living thing:

Kindness is the key to a happy life. It is a mental state of being, rather than an action. We should approach everything we do, every situation we encounter, with kindness. One way to help create kindness is to understand that we are all on the same spiritual journey, even if we are at different stages of that journey. Being a kind person means being kind to ourselves, as well as being kind to others. For this reason, we must not be so kind to others that we allow them to take advantage of us. Living with kindness gives us the ability to honor what we have in life.

Chapter 3: Healing with Reiki

Does Reiki work? Yes, by all means, Reiki does work. Reiki functions by flowing through the areas in the body that have energy blocks and flooding them with positive energy. The vibrations of the energy field inside and around the body cause the negative energy to dislodge and break free, clearing the energy pathways so that life force energy can once again flow through the body unhindered.

There are many people who are skeptical about Reiki's validity. Some are skeptical to the point that they won't even try it to see if it's possible that it might work. There are also people who are skeptical, but not closed to the possibility. They might even be open-minded and intrigued enough to try Reiki. Then there are the people who are incredibly open-minded and will happily try Reiki. Regardless of who tries it, Reiki will work on everyone, even if they don't believe it did anything for them.

The Benefits of Reiki

Reiki is often described as the power of love or a love-based energy. The only limit to the healing powers of Reiki is that which we construct. Anyone, anywhere, anytime can practice or be treated with Reiki. It is safe and the benefits of the treatment are numerous. These benefits include:

- Improving the immune system
- Heightening intuition
- Improving vitality
- Treating the symptoms and causes of illness and disease

- Calming and relieving stress
- Helping create balance in all areas of life

In addition, Reiki:

- Provides unconditional love
- Complements other traditional and conventional methods of healing
- Does not conflict with any religious or spiritual beliefs or paths
- Is available to you at all times

Reiki can also clear away negative energy that builds up in the body over time. Even when you are a relatively positive person, you are interacting with many different people every day and many of those people give off negative energy in the form of negative attitudes, thoughts, and emotions. It is very difficult to avoid having those negative energies influence your energy and your aura. Negative energy can also invade your personal home or office space or any other space in which you must spend time and sometimes this negative energy needs to be cleared away.

Anytime you feel negative energy within yourself, you can perform a self-healing session. Letting Reiki flow through you will allow you to cleanse the negative energy from you. The more you use Reiki on yourself, the more impervious you will be to negative energy. You can also use Reiki energy to clear the negative energies from any space.

The best way to understand what Reiki can do for you and how it feels is to experience it for yourself. A full-body treatment is the best way to do this. While this book does talk about the basics of becoming a Reiki practitioner, it is advised that you take the time to have at least one Reiki treatment before you decide to take the practitioner training. Even with one treatment, when Reiki is introduced to your body, you will find positive changes occurring. When you are ready to attune to Reiki and train as a practitioner, you will experience more positive changes at varying levels of subtlety. These changes will all be of benefit throughout your life.

Reiki is Completely Safe

There is absolutely no risk of harm when performing a Reiki treatment, either to the recipient or the practitioner. Reiki is just the natural energy of the universe. It's already present in and around everything. It is also important to understand that the practitioner is not *applying* Reiki to the recipient of the treatment. The practitioner is not guiding the energy at all, but simply acting as a conduit for it. The energy goes only where it is needed and only provides as much as is needed.

The only danger in receiving Reiki lies in the potential for the recipient to use Reiki to treat a serious illness or injury to the exclusion of other forms of treatment and healing. It is incredibly important to always follow your health care provider's advice concerning your health. Using Reiki as a supplementary treatment and as a general stress-reducer and healing force will help you stay healthy and aid in the healing

31

process for illnesses that require medical intervention. Reiki should never be used as a replacement for these medical treatments.

Reiki can be performed on anyone. You can give yourself Reiki treatments and you can give Reiki treatments to others. While it is the most effective to provide a Reiki treatment to someone who is physically present, it is also possible to perform distance-healing. Let's start with the idea of self-treatment.

Preparing for a Treatment Session

When you are going to give a Reiki treatment, you need to prepare in advance so that both you and the space you use will be ready to create the atmosphere you desire.

Personal Preparation

When it comes to preparing yourself, a good first step is to follow the Reiki Principles discussed above. If you live your life in this manner on a daily basis, you will always have positive energy.

You also want to ensure that your body is well prepared for Reiki. Prior to giving a treatment, you should be bathed and clean and dressed nicely in loose-fitting clothes, ideally made out of natural materials, such as wool or cotton. Be sure you are well groomed and your teeth are clean and do not wear any scented products.

You will also want to clean your aura when you are about to give a Reiki treatment. There are a few ways to accomplish this, the first of which is to simply clean your hands with cool water and run your wet finger through your aura as if you are combing it. Another option is to use either owl or turkey feathers in a sweeping motion through your aura.

Finally, you can do a smudge, which is a cleansing technique from the Native American tradition. When you smudge your aura, you burn a bundle of any combination of white sage, cedar, sweet grass, and lavender, fanning the smoke around and through your aura.

Spending some time in the sun every day, even if you are just sitting in a window, is a good way to cleanse and revitalize your body. If you are outside, then be careful you don't endanger yourself by being exposed to the sun's harmful rays for too long. If you live somewhere where you don't get much sun during certain times of the year, then you can use a full spectrum lamp that is designed to provide people with the benefits of sunlight.

Finally, always make sure you eat a well-balanced, healthy diet. You must have a healthy body to be able to effectively practice Reiki. Eating smaller meals more often is best and eating whole foods as close to their natural state as possible is ideal. This means no refined or fast foods and little or no sugar. The day you are going to give a Reiki treatment, eat light and avoid caffeine and alcohol for a minimum of 24 hours before the treatment begins. You should also drink plenty of water every day to help flush toxins from your body.

Preparing the Space

When it comes to preparing the space in which you perform your Reiki treatments, the best scenario is to have a space that is completely dedicated to Reiki. This might be a room in your home or an office dedicated to your Reiki practice.

If you have to set up a temporary area each time you give a Reiki treatment, then any and all distractions should be eliminated or minimized. Turn off the phone and all electronics in the room. Assure your Reiki recipient that your attention will be only on the session.

In order to offer Reiki treatments, you will need to invest in some specialized equipment and supplies. These include:

- Massage table
- Face rest
- Bolster
- Chair
- Pillows
- Blanket
- Linens
- Tissues
- Wastebasket
- Bottled water

Meditation and Focus

A few words about meditation and focus are beneficial here. Meditation offers numerous benefits on a mental, emotional, spiritual, and physical level. Just some of these benefits include:

- Reduces stress, depression, and anxiety
- Improves attention span
- Slows the aging process
- Improves sleep
- Boost the immune system
- Boosts metabolism
- Helps the brain function better
- Gives you more energy
- Makes you happier and feel more connected
- Lowers blood pressure
- Increases serotonin levels

The point of meditation is to quiet the mind and improve its ability to focus and focus is a key component in Reiki. One form of meditation often performed by Reiki practitioners is called Gassho meditation. This form of meditation has the practitioner sit in a comfortable position with the hands held in prayer position in front of the heart. Then you close your eyes, inhale Reiki through your nose and exhale it through your entire being on every level, including physical, emotional, mental, and spiritual.

This meditative practice can be accompanied by drawing one of the Reiki symbols on your body before you begin, listening to soothing music, chanting a mantra, focusing on a goal, asking for guidance, or simply visualizing the flow of Reiki through your body.

The benefits of Gassho meditation are:

- It quiets the mind.
- It helps you be in the present moment, in the "now."
- It helps you self-heal.
- It helps you shift your awareness to the flow of energy and how the energy works with you and your body.

By practicing meditation, either Gassho or another form, you will increase your ability to focus and it will ultimately help you become a better Reiki practitioner. Besides, meditation's innumerable health benefits are worth incorporating meditation into your life!

Chapter 4: Self-Healing with Reiki

If you are attuned and properly caring for yourself, then you should be a relatively healthy person. However, Reiki can be used to lower stress, produce a calming effect, and improve your overall balance, even when you are well. It is important to make self-healing treatments a regular part of your self-care schedule. As a new Level I practitioner, you should do a full-body treatment daily for the first four to six weeks. This will help promote balance within you. After this, you can do one or two full-body treatments each week.

It is very important that you make the time to give yourself full-body treatments. Determine what time of the day works best for you and stick to it. If you're an early riser, do it first thing in the morning before you move on with your day. If you are a night owl, perhaps it is better to do it at the end of the day. For many, midday is best. It is also ideal to do your Reiki self-treatments when you are alone and you have a relaxing, quiet atmosphere.

If you absolutely cannot schedule time for a regular full-body treatment, then at least do a partial treatment. You can do this on the go if you must, even if you are on the subway or in your office between meetings. Just try to find as relaxing a time and place as possible to perform your treatment.

Hand Placement

Before placing your hands for Reiki treatment, remove all jewelry form your fingers and wrists. You will hold your hands so that there are no gaps between your fingers and thumbs.

When you place your hands on your body, be sure not to apply any pressure. Pressure is not what channels the energy. As soon as you lightly place your hands on your body, the energy will automatically begin to flow.

For each full-body treatment on yourself (or someone else when treating others), you must begin at the face and work your way down the body. Each hand position should be held for five minutes, which will help ensure that each area of the body gets a balance of energy. There are 12 hand placements you will go through for each full-body treatment. These are as follows:

The face
The palm of your hands should rest on the sides of your face and your fingers should gently cover your eyes with the fingertips resting on your forehead. Make sure your nose and mouth are not covered as you do not want to obstruct your breathing.

The top or crown of the head
Place the palms of your hands on each side of your head, above your ears, and allow your fingers to go up your head. Your fingertips should meet at the very top of your head.

The back of the head
Place both hands, palms down, on the back of your head, one above the other. The lower hand should be just above the nape of your neck.

The chin and jaw

Place your hands so that they cup your chin and jaw. The inner surface of your wrists should be touching and your fingertips should be gently resting on your earlobes.

Neck, collarbone, and heart
Your right hand should be placed so that you are gently grasping your throat. Your thumb will run along the right side of your neck, below your jawline, and your fingers will wrap around the left side of your neck. Place your left hand on your chest between your collarbone and your heart.

Ribs
Bend your elbows slightly and place your hands on your rib cage just below your breasts. Ensure your fingertips are gently touching.

Abdomen
Bend your elbows slightly and place your hands on the area of your solar plexus, which is slight above your navel. Again, your fingertips should be lightly touching.

Pelvic bones
Place your hands over your pelvic bones, right over the right pelvic bone and left over the left. Ensure your fingertips are lightly touching in the middle.

Shoulders and shoulder blades
Reach backward over the tops of your shoulders and place each hand on your shoulder blades. This might be a difficult reach for some people. If you can't reach, then reach as far as you can. If you can only reach the tops of your shoulders, then rest your hands there.

Mid back

Reach your hands around your sides and behind you. With bent elbows, place your hands on your mid back. If you can reach far enough around, ensure your fingertips are gently touching.

Lower back

Reach your hands around your sides and behind you. With your elbows bent, place your hands on your lower back. If you can reach far enough, ensure your fingertips are gently touching.

Sacrum

Reach your hands around your sides and behind you. With your elbows bent, place your hands on your sacral area, which is at the base of your spine, right above your buttocks.

Potential Difficulties

If you are unable to reach or have difficulty reaching some of the hand placements, particularly in the back, then you can skip them or hold them for fewer than five minutes. You may or may not feel anything when you are treating yourself. If you don't, remember that doesn't mean the Reiki treatment isn't working. Keep doing it. Some people do feel shifts in their energy and various sensations as described in Chapter 1.

If you find it difficult to focus or concentrate, try closing your eyes. You can also use visualizations to help you. You can visualize water flowing from a tap as you place your hands. Reiki flows from your hands in much the same way water flows from a tap. The only difference is that while the flow of the water is controlled by a spigot, the flow of Reiki is controlled by the needs of the recipient. The greater the need for healing energy, the more quickly the energy will flow.

Track Your Progress

As you go through your Reiki self-treatments, it is a good idea to track your progress. In this way you will learn more about how the treatments work, how they affect you, and what you can tell others to expect based on your experience. Of course, your experience won't necessarily be the same as theirs, but your experience provides a guideline from which to draw.

Every time you perform a self-treatment, record your experience. You can do this in any way that feels best for you. If you prefer to journal, you can record your experiences in that manner. Perhaps you are a more analytical type, in which case it might be better for you to record your experiences in a chart or a table. Regardless of how you choose to record your self-treatment experiences, you should include the following information:

- Date of treatment
- Type of treatment (full-body or partial)
- Reason for treatment (especially if there is a particular issue, such as an area of pain or a more serious health concern)
- Other treatments being done for the issue
- The results of the Reiki treatment

If you find yourself avoiding self-treatment, you need to get to the root of why. It could be something as simple as not having enough time, which likely means your schedule is packed too full. It could also be for a deeper reason, such as subconsciously believing you are not worthy of the healing and love. But think about this. How can you provide healing and loving energy to others if you don't feel *you* deserve the same? Please do NOT avoid treating yourself.

Chapter 5: Healing Others

The very first and most important rule of treating others with Reiki is to foster an atmosphere of open communication between the practitioner and the recipient. You and your recipient need to work as a team to improve the recipient's health and wellbeing. This means you each have to help create a relaxing environment in which you trust each other. Only in that way will either of you feel safe enough to truly let go and give yourselves to the treatment.

Before Treatments Begin

Taking the time to communicate with each other prior to beginning Reiki treatments is critical. First of all, you will be able to explain what Reiki is, how the treatments work, and what the recipient can expect. You can also answer any and all of your recipient's questions and soothe any anxiety or apprehension the recipient might feel. This is particularly important considering that Reiki involves touching the recipient's body, something that might be a source of anxiety for that person. By starting to establish that open communication we just spoke of and starting to build trust immediately, you can waylay these concerns.

During this time of initial communication, you and the recipient will get a feel for each other's personality and develop a rapport. If for some reason the rapport feels off for you, you can refer the recipient to another practitioner. You should also encourage the recipient to find another practitioner if things don't feel right for her. After all, not everyone who walks through your door will jive with you and vice versa. Sometimes two people simply aren't a good match and their personal energies don't complement each other.

You will also outline how the treatments will go. You can tell the recipient the following information:

- How long each session will take
- How the recipient can prepare for the treatment (how to dress, what to eat, etc.)
- What the recipient will do during the treatment
- Whether it is fine to talk or fall asleep during the treatment (talking might be distracting, but sleeping is just fine)
- How to breathe during the treatment
- How and where you will touch the recipient during the treatment
- How the treatment will end
- What the recipient should do after the treatment

During the initial consultation, you will want to get a good feel for why the recipient is seeking Reiki treatment. Perhaps she is simply curious and wants to try it. Maybe she wants a different way to manage stress or perhaps she has a more serious illness or emotional imbalance she wants to treat. The key here is to determine the recipient's goals for the Reiki treatments and then establishing a plan to reach those goals. You and the recipient *must* be on the same page when it comes to the reason for the Reiki treatment. In order to help determine the intentions of the recipient and set a focus for the Reiki treatments, you can ask a few questions during your initial consultation, such as:

- How do you feel?
- Do you have any physical or mental health concerns?
- Do you have any emotional concerns?
- Have there been any major changes in your life recently?
- Are you a happy person?
- What do you expect or hope to achieve from this treatment?
- Do you sleep well?
- Do you worry excessively?
- What are your emotional triggers?
- What are your most concerning fears?

Remember, these questions are examples. You can ask any questions that will gently probe the recipient and help you work together to determine a focus for the treatment.

Hand Placements

The hand placements used when treating others are done on the same areas of the body as those for self-treatment. However, because you are laying your hands on someone else, rather than yourself, you will position them slightly differently.

The first four Reiki hand positions will require the recipient to lie on her back on the massage table. You will need to sit on a chair behind the recipient's head.

The face

The palm of your hands should rest on the recipient's forehead while the fingers gently lay over the eyes and the fingertips gently rest on the recipient's cheeks. Your thumbs should meet in the middle of the forehead. Make sure you do not cover the nose and mouth of the recipient, as you do not want to obstruct her breathing.

The top or crown of the head
Place the heels of your hands on the top of the recipient's head so that your inner wrists gently touch at the top of the head. Your palms and fingers will wrap down along the side of the head with your fingertips gently resting on the tops of the recipient's ears.

The back of the head
Slide both hands underneath the recipient's head so that her head is resting in the palms of your hands and the back of your hands are resting on the massage table.

The chin and jaw
Place your hands so that they cup the recipient's chin and jaw. Your fingertips will touch beneath the recipients chin and the hands will wrap around the jaw until the heels of the hands each rest on or just below the earlobes.

Neck, collarbone, and heart
For this position, you might be able to remaining sitting behind the recipient's head, but if your arms are not long enough to reach the recipient's throat and chest, then you will need to shift your chair to the side of the recipient. Your right hand should be placed so that you are gently grasping the right side of the recipient's throat. If the recipient is not comfortable with you touching her throat, then you can allow your hand to remain

just above the throat. Place your left hand on the recipient's chest, directly over her heart.

Ribs
For this and the next two positions, you will need to be seated at the recipient's side. Place your hands on the recipient's rib cage just below her breasts.

Abdomen
Place your hands on the area of the recipient's solar plexus, which is slight above her navel.

Pelvic bones
Place each of your hands over the recipient's pelvic bones.

Shoulders and shoulder blades
This and the remaining positions are done with the recipient lying on her stomach and you seated to her side. Place your hands on the recipient's shoulder blades.

Mid back
Place your hands across the middle of the recipient's back.

Lower back
Place your hands across the recipient's lower back.

Sacrum
Place your hands on the recipient's sacral area, which is at the base of her spine, right above her buttocks.

Set Your Boundaries

As you become accustomed to performing Reiki treatments and the people you know and treat tell the people they know about you, word will spread. This is most certainly good for business. In fact, all businesses rely on word-of-mouth. However, Reiki is not something you do for anyone, anytime, anywhere. If requests from people start flooding in, you will have to step back, assess your own feelings and what you want to accomplish with Reiki, and set some boundaries.

You never have to treat someone if you don't want to. Sometimes you might feel pressured into doing a treatment, but you still don't have to. Even if a friend or co-worker shows up at your home with an ill relative, asking you to do a treatment right then and there, you can still say no.

You can also refuse to do treatments for free. While you are trying to be of service to others, you have a life to live, bills to pay, and you need to eat. Charging a fee for your services is reasonable. If anyone you know asks you to perform a treatment, but doesn't want to pay, you can refuse. Politely, of course!

As a practitioner, you might also encounter situations in which you are entrusted with sensitive information regarding someone's state of health, a family situation, or relationship issues. If you are comfortable with these types of situations, then by all means carry on with treatments, but be sure to keep that information confidential.

Chapter 6: Distance Healing

It is possible for Reiki treatments to be given at a distance. This is akin to saying a prayer. A practitioner who does a Reiki treatment at a distance will direct the healing energies to the recipient with the use of mental focus and visualization. Distance treatments must always be done only when the practitioner has the consent of the recipient. It is also important to remember that distance healing is done when hands-on healing is not possible, but it is not a proper replacement for hands-on healing.

Openness is Key

When performing distance healing, it is important that your focus remain on the recipient, but open in its intentions. Even if the recipient has a specific issue, it is best if you send the healing energy without setting limits on it. This way, the Reiki will be free to go where it is needed the most. At a distance, Reiki is more likely to affect the chakras and the aura of the recipient in the short-term, taking more time to affect the physical body.

Be patient. A distance healing session takes far less time (just a few minutes) than a hands-on session, but the effects can still be incredible, particularly if you send Reiki multiple times. If the recipient is open-minded, she is might very well feel when you have done a treatment and why you have done it.

The Reiki Symbols

When performing distance healing, the practitioner must make use of the Reiki symbols. These symbols are learned in Reiki levels II and III and are also used during attunement. The Reiki symbols are, in part, based on the Japanese Kanji writing system.

The Power Symbol

The Reiki Power symbol is Cho Ku Rei, which means "Place the power of the universe here." This symbol is used to boost the power of Reiki, which is why it is used in distance healing, to increase the power of the healing so that it will reach the recipient and have more of an effect. However, this symbol can be used during hands-on treatments as well, in order to increase your access to Reiki.

The best time to use this symbol during treatment is either right at the beginning, when it will increase the power of Reiki for the session, or at the end, when it will effectively seal off the flow of Reiki. The Power symbol can also be used to:

- Better focus Reiki into a specific area of the body
- Boost the power of the other Reiki symbols
- Clear a room of all negative energies
- Clean objects, such as crystals, of negative energies
- Bring protection from negative energies to yourself, those you love, your home, and other items that are important to you

When using the symbol, you can simply visualize it in front of you. You can also draw it, either in the air in front of you or on the object or person you wish to protect. Because this is a strong symbol of power, there are likely many more uses to which it can be put. You just need to use your imagination to find other uses for you and your Reiki practice.

The Mental/Emotional Symbol

The Reiki Mental/Emotional symbol is Sei He Ki, which means "God and man become one." This symbol is used when dealing with mental and emotional problems in the recipient, which are being recognized more and more as the root cause of many of our illnesses and maladies. The goal in using this symbol is to harmonize and bring balance to the recipient's mental and emotional state.

The use of the Mental/Emotional symbol is to promote peace and harmony while balancing the left and right hemispheres of the brain. It can be used very effectively to help with relationship issues and can help treat a number of psychological problems, such as sadness, depression, anxiety, and anger. Other uses for the Mental/Emotional symbol include:

- Memory improvement
- Helping to find items that have been misplaced or lost
- Aiding in weight loss
- Healing misuse or abuse of alcohol and drugs

The Mental/Emotional symbol has a close relationship with Yin and Yang, which is also symbolic of the left (Yin) and right (Yang) hemispheres of the brain.

The Distance Symbol

The Reiki Distance symbol is Hon Sha Ze Sho Nen, which means "No, past, no present, no future." As the name of this symbol implies, it is the ideal symbol to use when performing distance healing. It is independent of time and place and it is considered to be the most powerful of the symbols by many Reiki practitioners. The Distance symbol can:

- Facilitate karmic healing by accessing the life record of the recipient, releasing trauma and experiences from past and future lives
- Treat people who are far away by sending Reiki to them
- Direct Reiki to someone from across a room
- Send Reiki into the past or present to offer support or release trauma

The Master Symbol

The Reiki Master symbol is Dai Ko Myo, which means "Great Enlightenment." This symbol is incredibly powerful and is only to be used by a Reiki Master. This symbol essentially brings together the power of the three symbols discussed above and has the highest vibration of all the symbols, bringing Reiki healing to a very spiritual level. This level of healing affects the soul and healing the soul automatically heals the mental, emotional, and physical.

There are many ways to activate the power of the Master symbol. You can draw it with your palm, your finger, or your third eye. You can visualize the symbol. You can also spell the name of the symbol three times. The Master Reiki symbol:

- Facilitates Reiki attunement

- Boosts the connection between Reiki energy and the practitioner
- Heals the soul
- Heals disease and illness at the source
- Pulls negative energy from the body
- Increases the effectiveness of the other Reiki symbols
- Brings the recipient to enlightenment
- Increases psychic and intuitive abilities
- Charges crystals so they can be used in self-healing
- Improves the healing properties of herbs, homeopathic medicines, and tinctures
- Energizes the immune system
- Enhances personal growth and spiritual development

The Completion Symbol

The final symbol used by the Reiki Master is the Completion symbol, also known as Raku. This is another very powerful symbol that is used at the end of an attunement. The use of the Completion symbol is to ensure a clean separation of the teacher's aura from the aura of the student. Care should be taken when using this symbol, placing it gently between teacher and student. The symbol will also align the student's chakras.

Chapter 7: Reiki Attunement

Up to this point, you have enjoyed the benefits of Reiki as a recipient and you have decided that you want more. However, when you make the decision to become a Reiki practitioner, you will not simply be passively accepting Reiki into your body; you will be starting a wonderful new journey in life. This will be a journey of change and growth. You might be wondering two things at this point. One is whether anyone can be attuned to Reiki and become a Reiki practitioner. The answer to this is a resounding yes! Anyone can be opened to receiving and channeling the Universal Life Force energy that is all around us.

This brings up the second question. If everyone has the ability to tap into and channel Reiki, then why is an attunement or initiation necessary? This is absolutely a valid question. While every person has the ability to connect with Reiki and channel it, there are many who need to be opened to it before they can do so freely.

This attunement is performed by a Reiki Master, who already has the ability to channel Reiki with great power and precision. It is this Reiki Master who will help you open yourself to the power of Reiki. This is like, shall we say, unlocking the door and allowing Reiki to flow through in a way that the practitioner can channel. This is done by opening the crown chakra and palms and establishing a special connection between the Reiki student and the Universal energy.

Another way to look at this attunement is like an initiation. When you attend your attunement, you are beginning your journey as a practitioner of Reiki. You are making a conscious decision to commit to a life of helping others as a Reiki practitioner. There is something formal about an initiation that brings confidence to you and to your recipients that you are indeed a capable Reiki practitioner.

Choosing a Reiki Teacher

Before you get to your Reiki attunement, you need to choose a teacher. This must be done carefully. Not every person is compatible with every other person. Just as we discussed that not every recipient and practitioner are right for each other or should work together, the same can be said for student and teacher.

You will have to shop around, check the feel of each teacher you meet, determine whether there is a rapport and connection that would make this person a good teacher for you. And don't forget that the Reiki teacher is doing the same, sizing you up to see if you would be a suitable student. The partnership of student and teacher has to feel right to both participants.
There are a few questions you should ask yourself before short-listing the teachers you want to interview. These include:

- Does it matter if the teacher is male or female?
- How much are you willing or able to afford to pay for instruction?
- How far away from home are you willing to travel for classes?
- Do you have the time to devote to your training, including the daily meditation and self-treatments?
- Are you ready and willing to live a healthier lifestyle?

Once you have an idea of what you are looking for, create a short-list of the Reiki teachers you are considering and arrange to meet with each of them. Be prepared ahead of time with the questions you want to ask so that you will not waste the teacher's time or your own time. You might only have a few minutes in which to conduct this interview, so be thorough, yet efficient. The following questions are appropriate and relevant when interviewing a potential Reiki teacher:

- How long have you been a Reiki practitioner?
- How long have you been a teacher?
- Who was your teacher?
- Do you have a Reiki lineage? What is it?
- What Reiki system(s) do you teach?
- How many students are you currently teaching?
- How many attunements have you performed?
- How many attunements do you give to each student in each level?
- Do you provide booster attunements?
- What is your availability to students outside of class time?
- What subject matter/topics do you cover in class?
- Do I need any materials for class? What materials?
- How much hands-on practice will I get?
- What Reiki levels do you teach?
- Are you part of any Reiki groups?
- Will I receive certification once I complete your training?

Above all, trust your instincts when choosing a Reiki teacher. Lineage, the passing on of teaching and attunement from Master to student stemming from one of the original teachers, is not the most important thing. Most likely you will know pretty quickly whether the person you are talking to is someone you want to work with.

It is important to note here that there are opportunities to learn Reiki online. While many of these are legitimate opportunities to train with real Reiki Masters, they are not ideal. It is best, if at all possible, to find a local Reiki Master to teach you. This way, you will receive a hands-on attunement and face-to-face instruction.

Distance attunements are possible, but do not come without concerns. It is more difficult to know if you are compatible with the Reiki Master who is teaching you. You also miss out on class discussions and hands-on training. Only choose distance and online training if you truly have no other options.

Preparing for Attunement

Once you have found the Reiki Master you wish to have as a teacher and you have signed up for training, you need to prepare for your first and subsequent attunements. You will have better results from your attunement if you follow these guidelines:

- Do not consume meat, fish, or poultry or consume alcohol within the three days leading up to the attunement.
- Reduce or eliminate your consumption of caffeine in general and do not consume any caffeinated beverages on the day of the attunement. This includes coffee, tea, chocolate, and colas.

- Reduce or eliminate the consumption of sugar.
- Cut back or stop smoking (if applicable).
- Reduce or eliminate time spent watching television, listening to the radio, and reading newspapers.
- Meditate or sit in silence for an hour each day for at least one week before the attunement.
- Spend time in nature.
- Ensure you get a moderate amount of exercise.
- Follow the Reiki Principles (see Chapter 2).
- Try to be aware of what is going on around you, of subtle impressions, and consider what they mean.
- Get a good night's sleep the night before the attunement.
- Eat a nutritious breakfast the morning of the attunement.

The Attunement

The specific attunement process you undergo will depend on the Reiki system you are learning. We will discuss the Reiki systems in Chapter 9. For now we will discuss the general details of Reiki attunement.

Attunement is a bit mysterious. It's been kept that way on purpose. During attunement, the student must keep her eyes closed. The purpose behind this not to maintain the secretive nature of the attunement, but to ensure the student will be in a more relaxed, meditative state and experience fewer distractions. Reiki attunements for each Reiki level are as follows:

- Four attunements in Reiki Level I
- Two attunements in Reiki Level II

- One attunement in Reiki Level III

There is also a special attunement called Hui Yin that a Reiki Master can use on a student any time she feels it is necessary. This Hui Yin is a booster attunement that is given to a student or practitioner whenever there is a need to remove blockage and get Reiki flowing again.

The Attunement Experience

Every student experiences their attunement differently. However, it is a powerful spiritual experience for anyone who undergoes it. It is not uncommon for students who go through attunement to feel a change within them. Spiritual beings and guides might be present during attunement and students commonly find they experience visions, healing, personal messages, and memories from past life experiences. A student's psychic awareness can also be awakened or become more sensitive. During attunement, some students even remember being a Reiki practitioner in a past life.

Chapter 8: Training Levels

There are three levels of Reiki training that you can go through. You can choose to go through just Level I or you can go through two or all three levels. The traditional method of teaching the Reiki levels was that a student could not move on to the next level until she showed adequate proficiency in the preceding levels. It could take weeks or months, or even years sometimes, to move on to the next level. Many Reiki Masters still teach in this way and that is a good thing. However, there are Masters who teach differently, offering classes in which you can attune to and learn more than one level at a time.

The most important part of any class is the attunements the students receive. These attunements will always be a part of the students' lives. The material taught in each class might vary from teacher to teacher, but in general you will learn the same basic things. Each Reiki level takes you farther into the experience and power of practicing Reiki.

A few things that are beneficial to know and applicable to each level of Reiki are as follows:

- If you can find a teacher with small class sizes, that is best; there is more one-to-one instruction in these situations.
- Classes are often held in the Reiki Master's home.
- Don't be late for class; it's disrespectful.
- Wear comfortable, loose-fitting clothing to class, preferably made out of natural materials, such as cotton or wool.

- If your class is in a different town or city, it might be wise to arrange for a hotel room for the night. You don't really know how your first day of attunements and energy work will affect you.

Reiki Level I

This level of Reiki introduces the student to the practice of Reiki and prepares her to be able to conduct hands-on healing sessions with recipients. The training for Level I will be between 8 and 16 hours and this is often done over a period of two days. Classroom introductions will be made so that everyone begins to get to know each other and so each of you can explain why you are taking the class. There will likely also be a class overview.

The teacher will then pass attunements and teach the class over the course of the two days. There are traditionally four attunements, but some teachers give only one or two attunements. Students will learn the history of Reiki and the basic hand positions for both self-treatment and treating others. They will perform a self-treatment and will also perform and receive at least one treatment, working with classmates in pairs or in small groups.

Once the Level I training is complete, students will receive a certificate stating that they have successfully completed the training. At this point, they can offer hands-on treatments to recipients.

Reiki Level II

Level II Reiki training will boost students' power, giving them the ability to conduct distance healing. This is not training that was traditionally offered to just anyone who had done Level I training, but only to those who the Reiki Master felt was ready for the next step in their training. This means being ready on an emotional and psychological level and wanting to carry on with training for the right reasons, not just for the money or the status that might come with being a Reiki practitioner. Some Reiki teachers require that a period of at least 21 days has passed between the end of Level I training and the beginning of Level II training. Some teachers prefer as much as three months between the two levels.

If you are considering moving on to Level II Reiki training, you should be sure you are ready for it. There are a few questions you can ask yourself before signing up for classes that will help you determine how ready you truly are:

- Why do you want to take Level II training?
- Do you understand Reiki well on a basic level?
- Do you practice Reiki regularly, on yourself and/or others?
- Can you feel the energy coming through your palms when you administer Reiki?

Level II Reiki classes will be taught over a period of six hours, which are typically done in two three-hour sessions over the course of two days. Again, the classes will start off with a period of introduction. You will be able to share your experience with being a Level I practitioner and you will hear the experiences of others. This can be a very rewarding experience all on its own.

During the Level II classes there will be two attunements given (some teachers give only one), one on the first day and one on the second day. It is also during the Level II classes that students will be introduced to the first three Reiki symbols. Students will learn what each symbol is, what it means, and will practice drawing it. They are expected to memorize it between sessions. After the second attunement, students will practice sending Reiki treatments to each other across the room. They will also work with the symbols and play games that will help them gain a deeper understanding of the symbols.

Remember that the Level II Reiki training is a very fun class that typically has good energy. You are all already Reiki Level I practitioners, which brings good energy, and you will be able to spend time drawing and having fun with each other as you learn the symbols and how to use them.

At the end of the Level II training, students will again receive a certificate stating that they have successfully completed the Level II Reiki training and are now a Level II practitioner.

Reiki Level III

Level III Reiki is a bit different than the other two levels. It is divided into three parts and it takes longer to go through this training than the other two levels of training combined! The three parts of Level III training are:

Master Healer: This is the level at which the student has received the attunement and has the ability to heal at the highest possible level.

Master/Teacher: This is the level at which the student has received Reiki Master level attunement and has been taught the Master symbol. At this point, the student is able to attune Level I and Level II students.

Grandmaster: This is the level at which the student is able to attune anyone at any level of Reiki, including passing the attunement for Grandmaster.

These three parts or distinctions are not always clear because everyone who has attained Level III training is referred to as a Master. The Master/Teacher and Grandmaster levels are often offered by the Reiki Master when they feel the student is ready. These levels of Reiki training do not follow a set number of days or a set course, but rather is more of an apprenticeship during which the student learns how to teach other people and pass attunements.

Level III Reiki requires at least 40 hours of training that, when involving all three Master Level distinctions, is often given in eight-hour sessions over the course of five weeks. Here is a breakdown of what students will learn each week:

Week 1:
Students will go through introductions and will be given the details of the course. Each student will write out the goals they want to achieve during the course and will begin a journal, in which they will record all of their in-class and out-of-class

experiences. At this time the Reiki Master attunement will be given and students will learn the Master symbol.

Week 2:
Sharing of experience stories and goals occurs, particularly experiences that have occurred since the Master attunement was passed. Students learn how to plan and teach Level I classes and pass the first two Level I attunements. The attunement process will be practiced as homework and all Reiki symbols will be reviewed and memorized.

Week 3:
Students share their goals and experiences and begin to recite the history of Reiki. They also learn how to pass the third and fourth Level I attunements and begin to cover how to plan and teach Reiki Level II classes. Symbol work is important here, as the students must ensure they know them well enough that they can teach them to others. Homework will be to practice what they have already learned and begin to study how to pass Level II attunements.

Week 4:
Students share their goals and experiences and recite further Reiki history. They then learn how to pass both Level II Reiki attunements and work more with how to structure and teach the Level II class. Ethics are also discussed.

Week 5:
This is the final Level III Reiki class in which students begin with sharing goals and experiences. They also learn to pass the Master level attunements and how to structure and teach the Master Level class. At the end, students receive a certificate that

confirms they have successfully completed Level III Reiki training.

Final Thoughts on Training

When you take any levels of Reiki training, you will learn what you need to learn and you will have a certificate at the end of each level of training. However, you will need to actually work with Reiki in order to become truly skilled. The more you work with Reiki and give treatments to yourself and others, then more in tune with the energy and the practice you will become.

Think of a student training to be a doctor. They go through all the coursework, the gruelling hours of labs and textbook study, and even go into the hospital to observe and participate. However, after they have graduated, they still spend time in residency before they begin to practice on their own. This residency time allows the physicians to hone their skills.

Chapter 9: Reiki Systems

As we discussed in the introduction to this book, Reiki was discovered by Dr. Mikao Usui in Japan in the 1920s. There was only this one system to begin with and was the source of the system that Hawayo Takata brought back to the United States with her. Takata taught many people her system of Reiki and after her death there were 22 Reiki Masters who had trained under her. Two of these Masters, Takata's granddaughter Phyllis Lei Furumoto and Dr. Barbara Ray, claimed they were Takata's successors.

Furumoto claimed she was the direct lineage bearer of Reiki and helped found The Reiki Alliance. Dr. Ray claimed she was the Holder of the Intact Master Keys of Reiki, which had been passed from Dr. Usui to Dr. Jujiro Hyashi to Takata to Dr. Ray. Aside from the split between these Grandmasters, there have been others who have split off and formed their own systems. Let's take a look at the various systems in practice today.

Usui Reiki Ryoho

This is the original system developed by Dr. Mikao Usui and it is still the system that is practiced in Japan. The goals behind this system are to teach self-healing and spiritual development. There is a great focus on meditation and empowerments, which are used instead of attunements to open the student to the flow and channeling of Reiki.

Usui Shiki Ryoho

This system was based on the Usui-Hayashi lineage and focuses on the systems, the Reiki Principles, symbols, attunements, and the hand placements. This is the system that was brought to the United States by Hawayo Takata.

Raku Kei Reiki

This is a Reiki system developed by Arthur Robertson, whose lineage was Dr. Usui to Dr. Hayashi to Takata to Iris Ishikuro. He wished to enhance the Reiki experience by making use of kundalini breathing, the Breath of the Fire Dragon, Hui Yin, and various other practices and symbols originating in Tibet.

Usui/Tibetan Reiki

This Reiki system was created by Diane Stein and William Lee Rand. It is a combination of Usui Shiki Ryoho, Raku Kei Reiki, and Advanced Reiki Training. There are four levels of training in this system, Reiki I, Reiki II, and Reiki IIIa, and Reiki III Master. Additions to the system include meditations, psychic surgery, guides, healing attunement, crystal grids, and symbols from Tibet.

Other Systems

The four systems described above were the traditional Reiki systems in use, but there are so many more out there. It is beyond the scope of this book to describe them all, but here is a (not necessarily exhaustive) list of them:

- Authentic Reiki
- Tera Mai Reiki and Seichem

- Karuna Reiki
- Lightarian Reiki
- Transformational Reiki
- Wei Chi Tibetan Reiki
- Gendai Reiki-ho
- Karuna Ki
- Kundalini Reiki
- Reiki Tummo
- Shamballa Reiki
- Rainbow Reiki
- Violet Flame Reiki

Regardless of the tradition or system you train in, Reiki still comes from the same source and it will express itself differently with each practitioner because each practitioner will channel it based on their own personal vibrations and energies. Even two Reiki practitioners that learned from the same teacher and practice the same system will have differences in how they practice. It is these differences that have given rise to the many different traditions in use around the world. It is also these differences that have allowed the tradition of Reiki to evolve.

Conclusion: A Lifelong Ability

We have talked so much about what Reiki can do for others, but we have not come close to covering what it can do for you! Once you are trained in and attuned to Reiki, you will be able to channel if for life. There is no way you will ever lose the ability, although booster attunements might be needed if you don't practice Reiki frequently and the flow of energy slows or blocks up. Reiki offers you the opportunity to help others, which is, in and of itself, a rewarding way to live life. But it also offers you a new path to self-discovery and healing.

With Reiki attunement, you have unlimited access to the Universal Life Force energy that flows all around us. You will also ideally be living a very healthy lifestyle, one that compliments the use of Reiki. This will allow you to have a calmer, more balanced life. You will be able to monitor your chakras and ensure your energy centers do not become blocked and unbalanced. This will help you stay healthier physically, mentally, and emotionally.

Reiki is also something you can use to complement other forms of treatment. It can be used in addition to conventional medical treatments, to help alleviate symptoms and get at the root cause of illness and disease. It can be used before and after surgery as a way to soothe the body and emotions and speed the recovery time. It can be used by those who are already healthcare providers and caregivers. The U.S. government has even published papers that explore the benefits of using Reiki as a complementary therapy, and in particular, the benefits of nurses using Reiki therapy for themselves and their patients.

This is evidence of the effectiveness of Reiki and of its growing acceptance in mainstream medicine.

As you explore this new method of healing and invite Reiki into your life, take the time to savor each step of the journey. Be mindful of each new stage and record all of your experiences. Once you open yourself to Reiki, your life will never be the same again. It will be better than ever! And you will be able to pass those positive changes on to anyone who wishes to experience them. Helping people feel better and helping yourself live a positive life – there is no better feeling than knowing you have made these things happen.

Enjoy your journey with Reiki!

Made in the USA
Coppell, TX
12 June 2020